History, Analysis and Secret Tradition of the Tarot

By J. W. Brodie-Innes, Arthur Edward Waite and Manly P. Hall

Copyright © 2020 Lamp of Trismegistus. All rights reserved. No part of this publication may be reproduced or transmitted in any form or by any means, electronic or mechanical, including photocopying, recording, or by any information storage and retrieval system, without permission in writing from Lamp of Trismegistus. Reviewers may quote brief passages.

ISBN: 978-1-63118-431-445-1

Esoteric Classics

Other Books in this Series and Related Titles

Magical Essays and Instructions by Florence Farr (978-1-63118-418-5)

Ancient Mysteries and Secret Societies by Manly P. Hall (978-1-63118-410-9)

The First and Second Gospels of the Infancy of Jesus Christ by Thomas and James (978-1-63118-415-4)

Ancient Egyptian Mysteries and Hieroglyphics, Modern Freemasonry & Initiation of the Pyramid by various authors (978-1-63118-430-7)

The Gospel of the Nativity of Mary by St. Matthew (978-1-63118-448-2)

The Mysteries of Freemasonry & the Druids by Albert G. Mackey, Manly P. Hall &c (978-1-63118-444-4)

Essays on the Esoteric Tradition of Karma by William Q. Judge, Helena P. Blavatsky and Annie Besant (978-1-63118-426-0)

The Secrets of Enoch by Enoch (978-1-63118-449-9)

The Smoky God or A Voyage to the Inner World by Willis George Emerson (978-1-63118-423-9)

Rosa Alchemica, The Tables of Law & The Adoration of the Magi by William Butler Yeats (978-1-63118-421-5)

A Collection of Fiction and Essays by Occult Writers on Supernatural, Metaphysical and Esoteric Subjects by various (978-1-63118-712-4)

Cloud Upon the Sanctuary by K. Eckartshausen (978-1-63118-438-3)

The Feminine Occult by various authors (978-1-63118-711-7)

Thirty-One Hymns to the Star Goddess by Achad (978-1-63118-422-2)

Audio Versions are also Available on Audible and iTunes

Table of Contents

Introduction...7

Preface...9

The Tarot Cards
by J. W. Brodie-Innes...11

The Tarot and Secret Tradition
by Arthur Edward Waite...25

An Analysis of the Tarot Cards
by Manly P. Hall...33

Introduction

The word "esoteric" can be difficult to define. Esotericism in general can be seen less as a system of beliefs and more as a category, which encompasses numerous, different systems of beliefs. It's a bit of juxtaposition, since the word "esoteric" indicates something that few people know about, while the term itself broadly covers numerous philosophies, practices, areas of study and belief systems.

In a greater sense, Esotericism acts as a storehouse for secret knowledge, which is often considered ancient (by *tradition, if not by fact)*, passed down from generation to generation, in private. At various times in history, simply possessing the knowledge of some of these subjects, was considered illegal and a jailable offence, if discovered. This usually included such general topics as Alchemy, Qabalah, Hermeticism, Occultism, Ceremonial Magic, Astrology, Divination, Rosicrucianism and so on. Collectively, these areas of study were often referred to as the esoteric sciences.

Sometimes, the outer garment of a subject isn't esoteric, while what is hidden beneath it, is. As an example, Freemasonry isn't necessarily esoteric by nature (at *least not anymore)*, but certain signs, passwords and handshakes given to the candidate during their initiation, are in fact, esoteric, in the sense that they are hidden from the general public.

Today, in the twenty-first century, such topics are readily available at bookstores across the country, and numerous mainsteam publishers offer beginners guides and coffee-table volumes on many of these subjects, intended for mass appeal. Books like *"The Secret"* have turned previously arcane topics into household knowledge. All that being the case, however, it isn't to say that there still aren't buried secrets to uncover, ancient wisdom being ignored and forgotten mysteries to be explored. In fact, it is often that we are only able to further our own studies by standing on the shoulders of these disappearing giants.

Lamp of Trismegistus is doing its part to help preserve humanity's esoteric history by making some of these classics available to those students who are seeking to unearth the knowledge of these ancient colossi.

So, be sure to check other titles from our *Esoteric Classics* series, as well as our *Occult Fiction*, *Theosophical Classics*, *Foundations of Freemasonry* and our *Christian Apocrypha Series*. You can also download the audio versions of most of these titles from iTunes or Audible, for learning on the go.

Preface

A brief note to explain the contents:

In addition to the thoughtful and educational piece by Manly P. Hall, something that you can always except from a writer of his caliber, what this small collection contains is a Tarot article by J. W. Brodie-Innes followed by a direct response from Arthur Edward Waite.

Both Waite and Brodie-Innes were members of the *Hermetic Order of the Golden Dawn*. As well, both men were contemporaries and writers. Based on the vast output of books, articles, reviews and more, that Waite left behind, in hindsight it's apparent that Waite often had an adversarial relationship with other writers of his day. It's difficult to tell if his constant need to respond to other writers was due to a thin skin, a need for constant validation or perhaps he simply disliked having his academic scholarship challenged with opposing theories or maybe he simply wanted to be viewed as the only real authority on all matters esoteric, during his time on Earth. In this instance, both men were regular contributors to the English periodical *Occult Review*, run by Ralph Shirley. The essay presented here, by Brodie-Innes, first appeared in the February 1919 issue, and not to be left alone, there was an immediate response article published in the same magazine, the following month, written by Waite. This is the first time since their original publication that both of these essays have been reprinted together.

It's also interesting to note that in his response article, Waite recycled the title of the essay from a chapter title in his 1910 seminal work *The Pictorial Key to the Tarot*; although, the article itself appears to be unique and not just a self-plagiarized repurposing of previous writing, which he was sometimes known to do. In fact, the term "secret tradition" is a term that can be found semi-regularly being used in titles, throughout Waite's entire writing career. Other examples of this phraseology used in his titles are "The Hidden Church and a Secret Tradition," "The Secret Tradition in Freemasonry," "Traces of a Secret Tradition in Christian Times," "The Secret Tradition in Goetia," "The Secret Tradition in Alchemy," "Studies in Mysticism and Certain Aspects of the Secret Tradition" as well as others. And, even when not including the phrase in his title, it was a theme he regularly explored throughout his life.

The Tarot Cards

By J.W. Brodie-Innes

The strange, weird-looking cards known as the Tarot, with their bizarre designs, have interested and puzzled archaeologists, mystics and occultists for over a century; and many books have been written, from ponderous and learned tomes to popular manuals, from M. Court de Gebelin's *Monde Primitif* in 1781 to Mr A.E. Waite's *Key to the Tarot* in 1910. Yet the mystery remains unsolved. What was their origin? What do they mean? Are they primarily an occult treatise told in hieroglyphics, or merely the implements of a game of chance or skill, used as an afterthought for purposes of divination? Was their origin Egyptian, or Indian, or Chinese, or some as yet unguessed source? There is no reliable evidence, though there is plenty of bold assertion. The fact remains that we know they existed in the fourteenth century, and prior to that they are wrapped in impenetrable obscurity. Having read all the books, I could get access to on the subject, and studied many theories and speculations, I finally arrived at the Scottish verdict of 'Not proven'. Under these circumstances I should hesitate to intrude into the distinguished, circle of writers on the Tarot, even to the extent of an article, but that it so chances that I have one or two slight contributions to the study, which may be of interest to inquirers.

Many years ago it was my privilege to examine at leisure the magnificent collection of playing cards made by my friend,

Mr. George Clulow, one of the greatest living experts on the subject. That collection is now in America, where I am told it is the model for all such collections. The item that chiefly interested me was a splendid series of Tarot packs of all ages and all countries. And the point that struck me most was the continuance of the designs throughout, often it is true corrupted, where an ignorant engraver, copying from a copyist, and obviously unable to understand a symbol, had expressed it by an unmeaning flourish, or substituted a flower, or some object he was acquainted with, for an uncomprehended symbol. Thus the Bateleur who in the oldest examples had magical implements before him, came to have a shoemaker's tools. But by comparison of one pack with another these could easily be rectified. Occasionally some local or political cause had produced variations, but these also were detected without trouble. One such occurs in a modern French pack in my possession, where a strong antipapal bias has occasioned the substitution of the figures of Juno and Jupiter for the original La Papesse and Le Pape. Now and then some enterprising innovator has redrawn the entire pack to suit his own ideas of the symbology, as did the fantastic perruquier Alliette, who under the pseudonym Etteilla (*being his own name spelt backwards*) posed as an illuminated adept. But these have attained no vogue, and are now merely of interest to collectors, for the embody, not the ideals, whatever they may be, of the old Tarot, but only Etteilla's notion of what they ought to be. Discounting however these variants, the persistence of the designs through some five centuries, and many countries, is, to say the least of it, remarkable. And whether or no those designs are comprehensible, one feels thankful that the redrawers have not succeeded in displacing the old traditional patterns.

That the cards have long been used in Italy, and perhaps elsewhere, for a game is certain, and that before ever they were written about as occult emblems or implements of divination. Lord Mahon, in his *History of the Forty-Five,* quotes an English lady who met Prince Charles Edward in Rome in 1770 at the Princess Palestrini's, when he asked her if she knew the game of Tarocchi, and she spoke of his handling the Tarot cards and explaining them. But one may conclude from the designs that they were originally intended for more than this. As played in Italy today the 22 Atus or Trumps are often omitted, and many packs are sold without these. But taking the ordinary pip cards, if they were simply used for a game, the ancient designs, which have persisted through so many years and in divers countries, would seem meaningless. The numbers of pips as in the common English packs would be sufficient. Why, for example, should the two of pentacles have a serpent coiled round the two pips in the form of the algebraic symbol of infinity. And here we may say that those well- meaning writers who have redrawn the cards have gone on the wrong tack. Admitting that we have no evidence of the original meaning (*there may or may not be a secret tradition, I wish to make no assertion as to this*) it is surely the part of wisdom to preserve the ancient symbol as clearly as we can, and await enlightenment, rather than to assume a meaning, and form a new symbol consonant thereto, which may be miles away from the primitive intention.

This at all events was the thought that came to me on examining Mr. Clulow's wonderful collection, and noting the persistence of the designs, and the variants of which I have spoken.

With regard to the 22 Atus or Trumps the case is different. It would be impossible in the compass of a single article to go into all the various interpretations that have been put upon them, nor am I sure that it would serve any good purpose to do so. In the absence of evidence as to the intention of the original designer they must remain as merely the speculations of individual writers. But there is much to be said for the idea of Eliphas Levi that they were to be referred to the Hebrew alphabet. Students of the Qabalah, who are familiar with the symbology of the Hebrew letters, have often been struck with the correspondence of some of the Atus with some of the letters. There can be no doubt that these cards are hieroglyphics of some kind, though the meaning seems to be in dispute; but whether they represent a series, such as the history of the soul, or cosmical evolution, or the grades of training of an initiate, or a synthesis of all of these and possibly others, there seems no positive evidence, but a great wealth of speculation. The connection with the Hebrew alphabet would largely depend on the attribution, and as twenty-one out of the twenty-two cards are numbered, the position assigned to the card marked zero called *le Mat*, or the Fool, must be the crucial point; and as to this there is wide divergence among the commentators. The wise student will maintain an open mind, and wait for further evidence; Eliphas Levi appears to take one a certain distance, and then slams the door in one's face, but whether because he did not know, or whether, knowing the secret tradition, he was unable to tell more, who shall say? In any case all are agreed as to the fascinating quality of his work, and undoubtedly no one can read it without having his interest profoundly stirred in these ancient cards.

It is generally supposed that they were unknown in France, or at all events in Paris, prior to M. Court de Gebelin, who it is said, found and introduced them to the French occultists. This, however, may be doubted. I have in my possession a French Tarot of the early eighteenth century, a very interesting feature of which is that some of the cards have MS inscriptions of their meaning, and apparently the records of an experiment in divination, which from internal evidence would seem to be Pre-Revolution. This, so far as it goes, would support the theory that they were known in France before M. de Gebelin wrote about them. I would not, however, press this further than as a warning against too confident dogmatism concerning the date of the Tarot, and the history of its introduction into Europe.

The cards have been called the '*Tarot of the Bohemians*', and have often been popularly spoken of as the gypsy fortune-telling cards. As a fact, however, when gypsies lay the cards for the fortune of an inquirer it is the ordinary pack that is used, and it seems certain, as Mr. Waite points out, that the Tarot cards were known in Europe before the arrival of the gypsies. Moreover gypsy folklorists, with the exception of Vaillant, have very little to say about the Tarot.

The only evidence on this head that has come under my own observation was from a woman of pure Romani blood, whom I knew many years ago, a Mrs. Lee, but of what tribe I cannot say; she was reputed to be an Epping Forest gypsy, but she said herself that her people belonged to Norwood, and only left there when Norwood became a wilderness of villadom, and their old haunts were desecrated by the incursion of Cockney residents. She once showed me an old tattered and much thumbed Tarot pack, of the ordinary Italian design, and told me that these were the cards she used among her own people, but never for Georgios. She also gave me the principles of interpretation, not under any seal of secrecy, but with a general request that it should not be published, and this, needless to say, I have honorably observed. I may, however, state that it was a thoroughly logical and complete system, the four suits representing the four elements, and the four temperaments, and being judged according to their position. Thus wands representing fire and the sanguine temperament, a wand card occurring in a bad position would indicate danger from rash and hasty action, anger, or quarrelling; the same card in a good position would show noble and generous action, courage, energy, and the like. Curiously enough the numbers of the pips were interpreted on a system very much akin to the Pythagorean system of numbers, especially in regard to the occult meaning of odd and even numbers. Mrs. Lee laid particular stress on the arrangement of the pips on the cards, pointing out its similarity to the arrangement of spots on dice and dominoes. (*The connection of this with the Pythagorean system is obvious.*) In the light of this explanation the appropriateness of the serpent in the design of the two of pentacles is manifest.

Whether Mrs. Lee's explanations were common to the gypsy tribes, or merely a system of her own, I cannot say. She seemed to regard it as very private, and only shown to me as a special mark of favor.

The last time I saw Mrs. Lee was some twenty years ago at Yetholm, when the son of the late Queen Esther was crowned Gypsy King. Mrs. Lee was very contemptuous of the Yetholm gypsies - 'Tinker trash,' she said, 'not a hundred words of Romani among the lot.' This, however, may well have been the prejudice of a different tribe.

I was interested to find that what she told me of the Tarot was well known to another friend of mine, the late Mrs. Florence Farr Emery, who herself claimed Romani descent, and had a great store of strange learning. She it was who first pointed out to me the correspondence of the interpretations of the pip cards with the Pythagorean system, greatly to my delight, for the meanings usually ascribed to the cards had seemed merely empiric, and founded on no system, as indeed are the meanings ascribed to cards by the ordinary type of fortune-teller today. More doubtful were Mrs. Emery's suggestions of Egyptian correspondences. She was a diligent student of Egyptology, though perhaps not quite as much of an authority as her friends claimed, and with natural enthusiasm was apt to see ancient Egypt everywhere.

Another unexpected gleam of light came to me from a friend of the late Charles Godfrey Leland, who told me that Leland had some special knowledge of a peculiar system of Gypsy Cartomancy, which for reasons known to himself he was not at liberty to divulge, and of a special pack of cards used by them. The friend who told me this had never seen the cards, but from the evidence of the Tarot pack shown me by Mrs. Lee it seems more than likely that these were in fact the Tarot cards, and that the interpretation thereof had been communicated as a secret to Leland. So then there appears to be a probability, in spite of the skepticism of the folklorists, that the connection of the Tarot with the gypsies may have a solid foundation in fact, and on this also we must await further evidence.

Meanwhile a guess may be hazarded that, although the cards arrived in Europe before the gypsies, they may yet have a common origin. Both the tribe and the cards arrived roughly about the same time, from an utterly unknown and mysterious source; and though the cards arrived first, there is no evidence to show that they did not come from the same origin. This will be a problem for future investigators, and a problem that I would humbly suggest is to be solved, not by negations, but rather by careful and open-minded examination of all the minutest traces of evidence available. It may be perfectly true to say there is no evidence of the Egyptian origin either of the cards or the people. But like other negations it takes us no farther. It may be right to deprecate the hasty dogmatism and superstition of those who proclaim loudly, on the very slenderest authority, that the secrets of the Universe have been laid bare, and the key to universal knowledge is in the hands of some certain mystic writer or teacher, who poses as a divinely inspired final authority and revealer of mysteries. There be many such nowadays, specially of the discredited German brand. But in this deprecation we should beware of falling into the opposite error, and because there is no proof, rashly assume that there is no evidence. It is by the patient examination of minute, almost invisible, and nearly obliterated traces, that true scientific investigation triumphs at length. There are traces, faint and infinitesimal it is true, of an Egyptian origin both of the gypsies and of the Tarot cards; and until some clearer indications of another origin are discovered it is wisdom to preserve these, and make the most of them, examine them with minutest care and search for others, meantime not neglecting any other clues pointing in any other direction. Above all, the careful examination of the designs of the cards, from the very earliest that can be discovered, with all their variants, must be an essential part of the inquiry. No good end can be served by redrawing the cards, however skillfully or artistically it is done. They will remain nothing but an evidence of the taste, and skill, and opinions of the artist, or his inspirer. But anyone who can in any way contribute to a reproduction of the original designs as they were, not as he thinks they ought to be, will do a real service to the study of the Tarot. Even the well-known and accepted symbols on the best of the current packs, well-drawn and colored, and well printed to replace the crude and poor examples which are the best we can get now, would be a boon to Tarot students, and would demand neither archaeological nor mystic learning.

In common with many Tarot students I welcomed Mr. Waite's little manual, and found therein as I expected, and as one always expects from his work, the result of careful research, set forth in graceful and elegant diction, an invaluable summary for those who have not the time or the patience, perhaps not the opportunity, to study the original works, of which he gives an excellent bibliography. But after all it carries one very little farther. *En passant* I was rather surprised that he should have taken the swords of the Tarot as the prototypes of clubs. So learned and accurate a writer must have had some authority for this statement, but none is given, and the obvious idea that in Italian swords is spadi, and the form of the pips in modern cards suggest a conventionalized drawing of the Roman broad sword, is not so much as alluded to. The original symbology as I have said remains unknown, and is open to any conjecture, but it must be said that the form of the club pip is singularly unlike a bludgeon or quarter staff. But if we take the suit of denarii, or pentacles, to represent earth forces, and suggest that money or coins might symbolize material powers, and that the clover or trefoil leaf, as a product of the earth, might also symbolize the earth forces, it might be as good symbology as the derivation of bludgeons from swords. In any case it seems to be generally assumed the cups are the prototypes of hearts, and scepters of diamonds, and if swords or spadi became spades, there is only left the correspondence of Pentacles with modern clubs.

There are then three ways in which we may regard the Tarot cards. Firstly the most obvious, as implements of a game of chance or skill, and this is only historically interesting. Secondly as a book of hieroglyphics, revealing, if properly interpreted, some great mystic truths. It may be some cosmogony, or history of evolution, either of the universe, or the human soul. And thirdly as a means of divination. Clearly the second of these depends entirely on our having the correct order of the cards; and as to this at present no light comes from antiquity, and modern authorities differ, as we have seen. The third, or divinatory use, depends on the chance laying down of the cards, the order in which they turn up after certain prescribed shufflings and cuttings by the querent. Mr. Waite inclines to the belief that the series of 22 Atus, or Trumps, were solely referred to the second of the above ways of regarding the cards; and the 56 pip cards, which he calls the lesser Arcana, were for no other use than for divination or fortune telling. This may be correct. Certainly there are examples of the Atus alone without the pip cards, and there are packs of pip cards sold now in Italy for the playing of Tarocchi with no Atus. Yet there are early examples in Mr. Clulow's collection of packs containing both, and clearly related. One form at least of the game is played with both, the Atus have a very special power justifying their name of trumps; and certainly also the system of divination shown to me by Mrs. Lee made use of both. I can only say that after examining all the evidence - that cited by Mr. Waite as well as some others - I have myself come to a different conclusion, but I consider the point still open to investigation.

As to divination or fortune-telling, there are many ways of laying out the cards; I have myself been shown over a dozen, and I am persuaded there are many more, some of them peculiar to individual diviners. The first method described by Mr. Waite has long been familiar to me. It was sometimes used among others by Mrs. Florence Farr Emery, but the divinatory meanings were entirely different. Rightly or wrongly they were logically formed by the combination of the general meaning of the suit with the mystic properties of numbers, which Mr. Waite apparently disregards. This divinatory meaning is broadly borne out by the old symbolic designs. The theory, therefore, is that the Tarot was in its origin a symbolic book, whose meaning can now only be remotely guessed at; that the original designers worked upon the fourfold division of all created things, whereof well-known examples are the four beasts of Ezekiel's vision, and of the Apocalypse, the four cherubim, the four archangels, the four letters of tetragrammaton, and many others; to which they added the mystic virtues of numbers, and upon each page of the book they placed a symbolic design still further to elucidate it. Each page on this theory would in fact form a chapter in the book, describing the good and evil influences operating from the spiritual on the material world. By the theory of divination the process of shuffling and cutting the cards according to the prescribed method would indicate the influences operating on the querent. We may perhaps compare the symbolic designs to the vignettes illustrating chapters in the *Egyptian Book of the Dead*.

If this theory is in any way correct it is obvious that it is of supreme importance to preserve by all means the ancient symbolic designs, and if possible to restore them to the state in which the original designers intended to set them forth. Archaeological research is continually bringing to light new and unexpected discoveries, and it may well be that any day some fresh evidence may be forthcoming on the forms of the Tarot, before the earliest that are now known, evidence that perhaps will without doubt connect these mysterious cards with one or other of the great races of antiquity and the great systems of philosophy or prove the fallacy of this idea. I trust that Mr. Waite may someday find time to tell us from whence he derived his interpretations, and the designs illustrating them.

Taking as an example the two of pentacles, of which I

have spoken before. Pentacles represent the earth forces - the material influences ruling our mortal life - and two according to the Pythagoreans is the number of divided councils, of Good and Evil, the first number to separate itself from the divine unity, hence associated with the dual nature of the serpent, or the two serpents, the serpent of the temptation, and the brazen serpent of healing lifted up by Moses in the wilderness, which was a type of Christ. Appropriately then in the old designs is the two of pentacles illustrated by the serpent coiled in the symbol of infinity. The interpretation may be true or false, I claim no special inspiration for it. It is merely a suggestion. But from whence comes Mr. Waite's dancing man? If he belongs to any of the old forms of the Tarot, or is in any way connected with the original designers, he is worthy of serious consideration. But one would like to know his origin and credentials. And the same remark applies to the other designs.

I am aware that my contribution is exceedingly small, but in tracing a path so obscure the faintest gleam of light may be of great value; I wholly agree with Mr. Waite in deprecating the attitude of those who assume a mighty air of mystery, and hint that an they would they could tell much. This is not the attitude of the real occult student. Those who know the secret tradition (*supposing there is one*) should either set forth their knowledge, if they may, and are not restrained by any pledges or honorable understanding, or should be silent; and those who have any interpretation to give should give their authority, or if the source be their own intuition or clairvoyance, should frankly say so. If all commentators would follow these simple rules of scientific investigation, we might be nearer to solving the two mysteries of the origin of the Tarot cards, and the origin of the gypsies, and either proving or disproving their alleged connection.

The Tarot and Secret Tradition

By Arthur Edward Waite

The Tarot is a puzzle for archaeology and it is also an intellectual puzzle. When the bare fact of its existence first became public in Europe, the seventy-eight cards were in use as a game and also as a method of divination and may have served these purposes for generations. Yet from the first to the last everyone who has taken up their study at all seriously has felt that the Trumps Major at least belonged originally neither to a game of chance nor to that other kind of chance which is called fortune-telling. They have been regarded as (1) allegorical designs containing religious and philosophical doctrine; (2) a veiled treatise on theosophy; (3) the science of the universe in hieroglyphics; (4) a keystone of occult science; (5) a summary of Kabalistic teaching; (6) the key of alchemy; and (7) the most ancient book in the world. But as these impressions have not been put forward accompanied by any tolerable evidence, it has been thought to follow in logic that Tarot cards belong to those arts in which they appear to have been used and to nothing else. In a little study of the Tarot, accompanied by the striking designs of Miss Pamela Colman Smith, and in its enlarged form as *The Pictorial Key to the Tarot*, I have intimated that a secret tradition exists regarding the cards. The statement is open to every kind of misjudgment, and it is time to correct a few exaggerated inferences which have arisen out of it. An opportunity seems given by the very interesting article of Mr. J.

W. Brodie-Innes, in the last issue of the *Occult Review*. He has reminded me of the whole subject and has mentioned one collection of cards which are a name only to myself. I will add to my remarks certain points of fact which are not mentioned in my books.

There are in reality two Tarot traditions, or -shall I say ?- unpublished sources of knowledge: one is of the occult order, and one is purely mystical. Each of the occult sciences has a golden side of its particular shield, and this is a mystical side, alchemy being a ready case in point. The art of transmuting metals was pursued secretly, and a long line of physical adepts claim to have attained its end, their procedure being recorded in books which *ex hypothesi* are clear to initiates, and to no one else. But there was another school or order of research speaking the same language of symbolisms, by means of which they delineated a different quest and a distinct attainment- both of the spiritual kind. I am led to infer that this spiritual or mystical school was later, though the peculiar veil of emblems used by Zosimus the Panopolite makes one inclined to suspend judgment. After the same manner there was Operative Masonry, but there came a period- placed usually towards the end of the seventeenth century- when there arose out of it that Emblematical Art which is so familiar now among us. In this case also there are vestiges of a figurative school at an earlier period, so again it is prudent to keep an open mind. Masonry is of course occult only in an attributed sense but- as a last example- there remains Ceremonial Magic and its connections, an occult art above all and in respect both of object and procedure about the last which might be supposed to have an alternative mystical aspect; but the fact remains.

The occult tradition of the Tarot is concerned with cartomancy in so far as it belongs to the manipulation and play of the cards for fortune-telling, but it has also a curious astrological side. The mystical tradition is confined to the Trumps Major, which I have termed the Greater Arcana in my two handbooks. The occult tradition leads no one anywhere, and its mode of practice in respect of the cards is- I am told- little, if anything, better than the published kinds- so far as results are concerned. I am not of course adjudicating on this question: as a mystic I should regard all such results as worthless. A prognostication which turns out amazingly correct is of no more consequence to the soul of man than another which proves far from the mark. The occult astrology of the Tarot has naturally its divinatory side, but it is not without traces of another and deeper intention. I should think it likely that the occult tradition will "leak out," as the saying is, one of these days, for it has passed through various hands which do not seem to respect it. The mystical aspect may be explained most readily as belonging to Kabalistic theosophy, and has proved illuminating to many on the mystic quest, provided that they happen to find help in symbolism. It is precisely the same here as it is in the Churches and secret societies like Masonry. Certain are aided by its pageants of ritual, while to others, they are little better than a rock of offence. The Eighteenth Degree of Rose-Croix is a hopeless adventure for those to whom ritual speaks no language, but so also is a Pontifical High Mass. Moreover, such good people would probably be well advised not to concern themselves about the mystical tradition of Tarot cards. They are not for such reason to be relegated to a lower scale and those of an opposite temperament have no warrant for assuming superiority. No one is further from God because the Ode Written in Dejection by Coleridge carries no message to his heart. There is no off or near side of the Kingdom of Heaven by these alternatives of inward character.

Such being the nature of the Tarot tradition in its two aspects there remains to be said that it has no information to offer on the time, place or circumstances of Tarot origins, nor on the question of its importation into Europe, supposing that it came from the East. There are of course expressions of opinion on the part of people who know the occult tradition, but I have not found that they are of more consequence than those of outside speculation. Speaking generally, my experience of all such traditions, when they happen to make a claim on history, is that they present mere figments of invention. The great mass of Masonic Rites and Orders have fraudulent traditional claims, and those of most Rosicrucian Societies are equally mendacious myths. Among notable exceptions are the *Regime Eccosais et Rectifie-* which includes the important Grades of Novice and Knight Beneficent of the Holy City- the Military and Religious Order of the Temple, the Order of Rose-Croix of Handover, and one mystical society which is referable in the last resort to the third quarter of the eighteenth century. As regards Craft Masonry it has worked out its own redemption by emerging from the Anderson period and its foolish fictions. If it be worthwhile to say so, by way of conclusion to this part of my subject, the Tarot tradition- whether mystical or occult-

bears no marks of antiquity. It would not signify how old they were if they had no other claim or value, while if they offer light on any questions of the soul, it matters nothing if they are of yesterday.

On their mystical side the Trumps Major offer most notable differences from any of the known recensions, including those of Miss Colman Smith. It will be obvious than I can offer no details; but Death, the Hanged Man, the Sun and Fool are among notable cases in point. I have said, now long ago, (1) that there are vague rumors concerning a higher meaning in the minor cards but (2) they have never yet been translated into another language than that of fortune-telling. Yet one knows not all that is doing nor always that which has been done, so it is well to add that I spoke within the measures of my own acquaintance- though I have had more than usual opportunities. In any case, the four suits of Wands, Cups, Swords and Pentacles have two strange connections in folk-lore, to one of which I drew attention briefly in The Hidden Church of the Holy Graal. So far as my recollection goes, I have not mentioned the other in any published work.

The four Hallows of the Holy Graal are (1) the Graal itself, understood as a Cup or Chalice, being the first Cup of the Eucharist; (2) the Spear, traditionally that of Longinus; (3) the Sword, which was made and broken under strange circumstances of allegory; and (4) the Dish of Plenty, about which the Graal tradition is composed, but it is understood generally as the Paschal Dish. The correspondence of these Hallows or Tokens with the Tarot suits will be noted, and the point is that albeit three out of the four belong to the Christian history of relics they have an antecedent folklore history belonging to the world of Celtic myth. This is a subject which I shall hope to carry farther one of these days. There are also the four treasures of the Tuatha de Danaan: these were the Sword of the Dogda, the Spear of Lug, the Cauldron of Plenty and Lia Fail, the Stone of Destiny which indicated the rightful King. I remember one of our folk-lore scholars, and a recognized authority on the texts of Graal literature, suggesting to me that something ought be done to link these pagan talismans with the Tarot suits, but I know as yet of no means by which the gulf of centuries can be bridged over. For the Tuatha de Danaan are of pre-Christian myth, but no one has traced Tarot cards earlier than the fourteenth century. The Tuatha de Danaan were mysterious beings of Ireland and divinities of Wales: some information concerning them will be found in Alfred Nutt's Voyage of Bran. They are said to be (1) earth-gods, (2) gods of growth and vegetation, (3) lords of the essence of life. They are connected with the idea of rebirth, usually of a god or hero.

I assume that an adequate survey of the vast field of folk-lore would produce other analogies, without appealing- like excellent old Court de Gebelin- to Chinese inscriptions or the avatars of Vishnu. It follows that the archaeology of the Tarot has made a beginning only and we know not whither it may lead us. Much yet remains to be done with antique packs, and I should be glad to follow up the reference of Mr. Brodie-Innes to the Clulow collection- now, as he mentions, in America. Whether it is in a public museum and whether there is a descriptive catalogue are among the first questions concerning it. One is continually coming across the titles of foreign books on Tarot and Playing Cards which might be followed up, not without profit, if we could get at the works themselves; but they are not in our public libraries. Were it otherwise, my bibliography of works dealing with the Tarot and its connections might be much extended. As regards packs, since the appearance of *The Pictorial Key* I have inspected a Jewish Tarot which has not, I think, been printed. It represents the black magic of divination- a most extraordinary series of designs, carrying message of evil in every sign and symbol. It is, so to speak, a Grimoire Tarot, and if it is not of French origin, the inscriptions and readings are in the French language. I have seen only the Trumps Major and two or three of the lesser Court Cards, but I understood that there is at least one complete pack in existence.

Mr. Brodie-Innes speculates as to the authority for my allocation of Tarot suits to those of ordinary playing-cards. Its source is similar to that from which Florence Farr Emery- one of my old friends and of whom I am glad to be reminded- derived her divinatory meanings mentioned by Mr. Brodie-Innes. The source to which I refer knew well of the alternative attribution and had come to the conclusion that it was wrong. In adapting it I was careful that no allocation should be of consequence to "the outer method of the oracles" and the meanings of the Lesser Cards. Nothing follows therefore from the attribution of Swords to Clubs and Pentacles to Spades. In my book on the Graal I had already taken the other allocation of Swords to Spades and Pentacles to Clubs. I cannot say that

I am especially satisfied by either mode of comparison. There is no connection in symbolism between a sword and spade, at least until the League of Nations turns all our weapons of offence into ploughshares and reaping-hooks. As little correspondence appears between so-called pentacles and clubs, but it is Hobson's choice. In the absence of a canon of criticism I should prefer to say nothing as to the mystic virtues of numbers in this connection.

An Analysis of the Tarot Cards

By Manly P. Hall

Opinions of authorities differ widely concerning the origin of playing cards, the purpose for which they were intended, and the time of their introduction into Europe. In his Researches into the History of Playing Cards, Samuel Weller Singer advances the opinion that cards reached Southern Europe from India by way of Arabia. It is probable that the Tarot cards were part of the magical and philosophical lore secured by the Knights Templars from the Saracens or one of the mystical sects then flourishing in Syria. Returning to Europe, the Templars, to avoid persecution, concealed the arcane meaning of the symbols by introducing the leaves of their magical book ostensibly as a device for amusement and gambling. In support of this contention, Mrs. John King Van Rensselaer states:

"That cards were brought by the home-returning warriors, who imported many of the newly acquired customs and habits of the Orient to their own countries, seems to be a well-established fact; and it does not contradict the statement made by some writers who declared that the gypsies--who about that time began to wander over Europe--brought with them and introduced cards, which they used, as they do at the present day, for divining the future."

Through the Gypsies the Tarot cards may be traced back to the religious symbolism of the ancient Egyptians. In his remarkable work, *The Gypsies,* Samuel Roberts presents ample proof of their Egyptian origin. In one place he writes: "When Gypsies originally arrived in England is very uncertain. They are first noticed in our laws, by several statutes against them in the reign of Henry VIII.; in which they are described as 'an outlandish people, calling themselves Egyptians,--who do not profess any craft or trade, but go about in great numbers…'" A curious legend relates that after the destruction of the Serapeum in Alexandria, the large body of attendant priests banded themselves together to preserve the secrets of the rites of Serapis. Their descendants (Gypsies) carrying with them the most precious of the volumes saved from the burning library--the Book of Enoch, or Thoth (the Tarot)--became wanderers upon the face of the earth, remaining a people apart with an ancient language and a birthright of magic and mystery.

Court de Gébelin believed the word Tarot itself to be derived from two Egyptian words, *Tar,* meaning "road," and *Ro,* meaning "royal." Thus the Tarot constitutes the *royal road to wisdom.* In his *History of Magic,* P. Christian, the mouthpiece of a certain French secret society, presents a fantastic account of a purported initiation into the Egyptian Mysteries wherein the 22 major Tarots assume the proportions of trestle boards of immense size and line a great gallery. Stopping before each card in turn, the initiator described its symbolism to the candidate. Edouard Schuré, whose source of information was similar to that of Christian's, hints at the same ceremony in his chapter on initiation into the Hermetic Mysteries. While the Egyptians may well have employed the Tarot cards in their rituals, these French mystics present no evidence other than their own assertions to support this theory. The validity also of the so-called Egyptian Tarots now in circulation has never been satisfactorily established. The drawings are not only quite modern but the symbolism itself savors of French rather than Egyptian influence.

The Tarot is undoubtedly a vital element in Rosicrucian symbolism, possibly the very book of universal knowledge which the members of the order claimed to possess. The *Rota Mundi* is a term frequently occurring in the early manifestoes of the Fraternity of the Rose Cross. The word *Rota* by a rearrangement of its letters becomes *Taro*, the ancient name of these mysterious cards. W. F. C. Wigston has discovered evidence that Sir Francis Bacon employed the Tarot symbolism in his ciphers. The numbers 21, 56, and 78, which are all directly related to the divisions of the Tarot deck, are frequently involved in Bacon's cryptograms. In the great Shakespearian Folio of 1623 the Christian name of Lord Bacon appears 21 times on page 56 of the Histories.

Many symbols appearing upon the Tarot cards have definite Masonic interest. The Pythagorean numerologist will also find an important relationship to exist between the numbers on the cards and the designs accompanying the numbers. The Qabbalist will be immediately impressed by the significant sequence of the cards, and the alchemist will discover certain emblems meaningless save to one versed in the divine chemistry of transmutation and regeneration. As the Greeks placed the letters of their alphabet--with their corresponding numbers--upon the various parts of the body of their humanly represented *Logos*, so the Tarot cards have an analogy not only in the parts and members of the universe but also in the divisions of the human body. They are in fact the key to the magical constitution of man.

The Tarot cards must be considered (1) as separate and complete hieroglyphs, each representing a distinct principle, law, power, or element in Nature; (2) in relation to each other as the effect of one agent operating upon another; and (3) as vowels and consonants of a philosophic alphabet. The laws governing all phenomena are represented by the symbols upon the Tarot cards, whose numerical values are equal to the numerical equivalents of the phenomena. As every structure consists of certain elemental parts, so the Tarot cards represent the components of the structure of philosophy. Irrespective of the science or philosophy with which the student is working, the Tarot cards can be identified with the essential constituents of his subject, each card thus being related to a specific part according to mathematical and philosophical laws. "An imprisoned person," writes Eliphas Levi, "with no other book than the Tarot, if he knew how to use it, could in a few years acquire universal knowledge, and would be able to speak on all subjects with unequalled learning and inexhaustible eloquence."

The diverse opinions of eminent authorities on the Tarot symbolism are quite irreconcilable. The conclusions of the scholarly Court de Gébelin and the bizarre Grand Etteila--the first authorities on the subject--not only are at radical variance but both are equally discredited by Levi, whose arrangement of the Tarot trumps was rejected in turn by Arthur Edward Waite and Paul Case as being an effort to mislead students. The followers of Levi--especially Papus, Christian, Westcott, and Schuré-are regarded by the "reformed Tarotists" as honest but benighted individuals who wandered in darkness for lack of Pamela Coleman Smith's new deck of Tarot cards with revisions by Mr. Waite.

Most writers on the Tarot (Mr. Waite a notable exception) have proceeded upon the hypothesis that the 22 major trumps represent the letters of the Hebrew alphabet. This supposition is based upon nothing more substantial than the coincidence that both consist of 22 parts. That Postel, St. Martin, and Levi all wrote books divided into sections corresponding to the major Tarots is an interesting sidelight on the subject. The major trump cards portray incidents from the Book of Revelation; and the Apocalypse of St. John is also divided into 22 chapters. Assuming the Qabalah to hold the solution to the Tarot riddle, seekers have often ignored other possible lines of research. The task, however, of discovering the proper relationship sustained by the Tarot trumps to the letters of the Hebrew alphabet and the Paths of Wisdom thus far has not met with any great measure of success. The major trumps of the Tarot and the 22 letters of the Hebrew alphabet cannot be synchronized without first fixing the correct place of the unnumbered, or zero, card--Le *Mat,* the Fool. Levi places this card between the 20th and 21st Tarots, assigning to it the Hebrew letter Shin. The same order is followed by Papus, Christian, and Waite, the last, however, declaring this arrangement to be incorrect. Westcott makes the zero card the

22nd of the Tarot major trumps. On the other hand, both Court de Gébelin and Paul Case place the unnumbered card before the first numbered card of the major trumps, for if the natural order of the numbers (according to either the Pythagorean or Qabbalistic system) be adhered to, the zero card must naturally precede the number 1.

This does not dispose of the problem, however, for efforts to assign a Hebrew letter to each Tarot trump in sequence produce an effect far from convincing. Mr. Waite, who reedited the Tarot, expresses himself thus: "I am not to be included among those who are satisfied that there is a valid correspondence between Hebrew letters and Tarot Trump symbols." The real explanation may be that the major Tarots no longer are in the same sequence as when they formed the leaves of Hermes' sacred book, for the Egyptians--or even their Arabian successors--could have purposely confused the cards so that their secrets might be better preserved. Mr. Case has developed a system which, while superior to most, depends largely upon two debatable points, namely, the accuracy of Mr. Waite's revised Tarot and the justification for assigning the first letter of the Hebrew alphabet to the unnumbered, or zero, card. Since *Aleph* (the first Hebrew letter) has the numerical value of 1, its assignment to the zero card is equivalent to the statement that zero is equal to the letter *Aleph* and therefore synonymous with the number 1.

With rare insight, Court de Gébelin assigned the zero card to AIN SOPH, the Unknowable First Cause. As the central panel of the Bembine Table represents the Creative

Power surrounded by seven triads of manifesting divinities, so may the zero card represent that Eternal Power of which the 21 surrounding or manifesting aspects are but limited expressions. If the 21 major trumps be considered as limited forms existing in the abstract substance of the zero card, it then becomes their common denominator. Which letter, then, of the Hebrew alphabet is the origin of all the remaining letters? The answer is apparent: Yod. In the presence of so many speculations, one more may not offend. The zero card--Le *Mat*, the Fool--has been likened to the material universe because the mortal sphere is the world of unreality. The lower universe, like the mortal body of man, is but a garment, a motley costume, well likened to cap and bells. Beneath the garments of the fool is the divine substance, however, of which the jester is but a shadow; this world is a Mardi Gras--a pageantry of divine sparks masked in the garb of fools. Was not this zero card (the Fool) placed in the Tarot deck to deceive all who could not pierce the veil of illusion?

The Tarot cards were entrusted by the illumined hierophants of the Mysteries into the keeping of the foolish and the ignorant, thus becoming playthings--in many instances even instruments of vice. Man's evil habits therefore actually became the unconscious perpetuators of his philosophical precepts. "We must admire the wisdom of the Initiates," writes Papus, "who utilized vice and made it produce more beneficial results than virtue." Does not this act of the ancient priests itself afford proof that the entire mystery of the Tarot is wrapped up in the symbolism of its zero card? If knowledge was thus entrusted to fools, should it not be sought for in this card?

If *Le Mat* be placed before the first card of the Tarot deck and the others laid out in a horizontal line in sequence from left to right, it will be found that the Fool is walking toward the other trumps as though about to pass through the various cards. Like the spiritually hoodwinked and bound neophyte, *Le Mat* is about to enter upon the supreme adventure--that of passage through the gates of the Divine Wisdom. If the zero card be considered as extraneous to the major trumps, this destroys the numerical analogy between these cards and the Hebrew letters by leaving one letter without a Tarot correspondent. In this event it will be necessary to assign the missing letter to a hypothetical Tarot card called the elements, assumed to have been broken up to form the 56 cards of the minor trumps. It is possible that each of the major trumps may be subject to a similar division.

The first numbered major trump is called *Le Bateleur*, the juggler, and according to Court de Gébelin, indicates the entire fabric of creation to be but a dream, existence a juggling of divine elements, and life a perpetual game of hazard. The seeming miracles of Nature are but feats of cosmic legerdemain. Man is like the little ball in the hands of the juggler, who waves his wand and, presto! the ball vanishes. The world looking on does not realize that the vanished article is still cleverly concealed by the juggler in the hollow of his hand. This is also the Adept whom Omar Khayyám calls "the master of the show." His message is that the wise direct the phenomena of Nature and are never deceived thereby.

The magician stands behind a table on which are spread out a number of objects, prominent among them a cup--the Holy Grail and the cup placed by Joseph in Benjamin's sack; a coin--the tribute money and the wages of a Master Builder, and a sword, that of Goliath and also the mystic blade of the philosopher which divides the false from the true. The magician's hat is in the form of the cosmic lemniscate, signifying the first motion of creation. His right hand points to the earth, his left holds aloft the rod of Jacob and also the staff that budded--the human spine crowned with the globe of creative intelligence. In the pseudo-Egyptian Tarot the magician wears an *uræus* or golden band around his forehead, the table before him is in the form of a perfect cube, and his girdle is the serpent of eternity devouring its own tail.

The second numbered major trump is called *La Papesse*, the Female Pope, and has been associated with a curious legend of the only woman who ever sat in the pontifical chair. Pope Joan is supposed to have accomplished this by masquerading in male attire, and was stoned to death when her subterfuge was discovered. This card portrays a seated woman crowned with a tiara surmounted by a lunar crescent. In her lap is the *Tora*, or book of the Law (usually partly closed), and in her left hand are the keys to the secret doctrine, one gold and the other silver. Behind her rise two pillars (Jachin and Boaz) with a multicolored veil stretched between. Her throne stands upon a checker-board floor. A figure called Juno is occasionally substituted for La Papesse, like the female hierophant of the Mysteries of Cybele, this symbolic figure personifies the Shekinah, or Divine Wisdom. In the pseudo-Egyptian Tarot the priestess is veiled, a reminder that the full countenance truth is not revealed to uninitiated man. A veil also covers one-half of her book, thus intimating that but one-half of the mystery of being can be comprehended.

The third numbered major trump is called *L'Impératrice*, the Empress, and has been likened to the "woman clothed with the sun" described in the Apocalypse. On this card appears the winged figure of a woman seated upon a throne, supporting with her right hand a shield emblazoned with a phoenix and holding in her left a scepter surmounted by an orb or trifoliate flower. Beneath her left foot is sometimes shown the crescent. Either the Empress is crowned or her head is surrounded by a diadem of stars; sometimes both. She is called *Generation*, and represents the threefold spiritual world out of which proceeds the fourfold material world. To the graduate of the College of the Mysteries she is the *Alma Mater* out of whose body the initiate has "born again." In the pseudo-Egyptian Tarot the Empress is shown seated upon a cube filled with eyes and a bird is balanced upon the forefinger other left hand. The upper part of her body is surrounded by a radiant golden nimbus. Being emblematic of the power from which emanates the entire tangible universe, *L'Impératrice* is frequently symbolized as pregnant.

The fourth numbered major trump is called *L'Empereur*, the Emperor, and by its numerical value is directly associated with the great Deity revered by the Pythagoreans under the form of the tetrad. His symbols declare the Emperor to be the Demiurgus, the Great King of the inferior world. The Emperor is dressed in armor and his throne is a cube stone, upon which a phoenix is also clearly visible. The king has his legs crossed in a most significant manner and carries either a scepter surmounted by an orb or a scepter in his right hand and an orb in his left. The orb itself is evidence that he is supreme ruler of the world. Upon his right and left breasts respectively appear the symbols of the sun and moon, which in symbolism are referred to as the eyes of the Great King. The position of the body and legs forms the symbol of sulphur, the sign of the ancient alchemical monarch. In the pseudo-Egyptian Tarot the figure is in profile. He wears a Masonic apron and the skirt forms a right-angled triangle. Upon his head is the Crown of the North and his forehead is adorned wit the coiled *uraeus*.

The fifth numbered major trump is called *Le Pape*, the Pope, and represents the high priest of a pagan or Christian Mystery school. In this card the hierophant wears the tiara and carries in his left hand the triple cross surmounting the globe of the world. His right hand, bearing upon its back the stigmata, makes "the ecclesiastic sign of esotericism," and before him kneel two suppliants or acolytes. The back of the papal throne is in the form of a celestial and a terrestrial column. This card signifies the initiate or master of the mystery of life and according to the Pythagoreans, the spiritual physician. The illusionary universe in the form of the two figures (polarity) kneels before the throne upon which sits the initiate who has elevated his consciousness to the plane of spiritual understanding and reality. In the pseudo-Egyptian Tarot the Master wears the *uraeus*. A white and a black figure--life and death, light and darkness, good and evil--kneel before him. The initiate's mastery over unreality is indicated by the tiara and the triple cross, emblems of rulership over the three worlds which have issued from the Unknowable First Cause.

The sixth numbered major trump is called *L'Amoureux*, the Lovers. There are two distinct forms of this Tarot. One shows a marriage ceremony in which a priest is uniting a youth and a maiden (Adam and Eve?) in holy wedlock. Sometimes a winged figure above transfixes the lovers with his dart. The second form of the card portrays a youth with a female figure on either side. One of these figures wears a golden crown and is winged, while the other is attired in the flowing robes of the bacchante and on her head is a wreath of vine leaves. The maidens represent the twofold soul of man (spiritual and animal), the first his guardian angel and the second his ever-present demon. The youth stands at the beginning of mature life, "the Parting of the Ways," where he must choose between virtue and vice, the eternal and the temporal. Above, in a halo of light, is the genius of Fate (his star), mistaken for Cupid by the uninformed. If youth chooses unwisely, the arrow of blindfolded Fate will transfix him. In the pseudo-Egyptian Tarot the arrow of the genius points directly to the figure of vice, thereby signifying that the end of her path is destruction. This card reminds man that the price of free will--or, more correctly, the power of choice--is responsibility.

The seventh numbered major trump is called *Le Chariot*, the Chariot, and portrays a victorious warrior crowned and riding in a chariot drawn by black and white sphinxes or horses. The starry canopy of the chariot is upheld by four columns.

This card signifies the Exalted One who rides in the chariot of creation. The vehicle of the solar energy being numbered seven reveals the arcane truth that the seven planets are the chariots of the solar power which rides victorious in their midst. The four columns supporting the canopy represent the four Mighty Ones who uphold the worlds represented by the star-strewn drapery. The figure carries the scepter of the solar energy and its shoulders are ornamented with lunar crescents--the Urim and Thummim. The sphinxes drawing the chariot resent the secret and unknown power by which the victorious ruler is moved continuously through the various parts of his universe. In certain Tarot decks the victor signifies the regenerated man, for the body of the chariot is a cubic stone. The man in armor is not standing in the chariot but is rising out of the cube, thus typifying the ascension of the 3 out of the 4--the turning upward of the flap of the Master Mason's apron. In the pseudo-Egyptian Tarot the warrior carries the curved sword of Luna, is bearded to signify maturity, and wears the collar of the planetary orbits. His scepter (emblematic of the threefold universe) is crowned with a square upon which is a circle surmounted by a triangle.

The eighth numbered major trump is called *La Justice*, Justice, and portrays a seated figure upon a throne, the back of which rises in the form of two columns. Justice is crowned and carries in her right hand a sword and in her left a pair of scales. This card is a reminder of the judgment of the soul in the hall of Osiris. It teaches that only balanced forces can endure and that eternal justice destroys with the sword that which is unbalanced. Sometimes justice is depicted with a braid of her own hair twisted around her neck in a manner resembling a hangman's knot. This may subtly imply that man is the cause of his own undoing, his actions (symbolized by his hair) being the instrument of his annihilation. In the pseudo-Egyptian Tarot the figure of Justice is raised upon a dais of three steps, for justice can be fully administered only by such as have been elevated to the third degree. Justice is blindfolded, that the visible shall in no way influence its decision. (For reasons he considers beyond his readers' intelligence, Mr. Waite reversed the eighth and eleventh major trumps.)

The ninth numbered major trump is called *L'Hermite*, the Hermit, and portrays an aged man, robed in a monkish habit and cowl, leaning on a staff. This card was popularly supposed to represent Diogenes in his quest for an honest man. In his right hand the recluse carries a lamp which he partly conceals within the folds of his cape. The hermit thereby personifies the secret organizations which for uncounted centuries have carefully concealed the light of the Ancient Wisdom from the profane. The staff of the hermit is knowledge, which is man's main and only enduring support. Sometimes the mystic rod is divided by knobs into seven sections, a subtle reference to the mystery of the seven sacred centers along the human spine. In the pseudo-Egyptian Tarot the hermit shields the lamp behind a rectangular cape to emphasize the philosophic truth that wisdom, if exposed to the fury of ignorance, would be destroyed like the tiny flame of a lamp unprotected from the storm. Man's bodies form a cloak through which his divine nature is faintly visible like the flame of the partly covered lantern. Through renunciation--the Hermetic life--man attains depth of character and tranquility of spirit.

The tenth numbered major trump is called *La Roue de Fortune,* the Wheel of Fortune, and portrays a mysterious wheel with eight spokes--the familiar Buddhist symbol of the Cycle of Necessity. To its rim cling Anubis and Typhon--the principles of good and evil. Above sits the immobile sphinx, carrying the sword of Justice and signifying the perfect equilibrium of Universal Wisdom. Anubis is shown rising and Typhon descending; but when Typhon reaches the bottom, evil ascends again, and when Anubis reaches the top good wanes once more. The Wheel of Fortune represents the lower universe as a whole with Divine Wisdom (the sphinx) as the eternal arbiter between good and evil. In India, the *chakra,* or wheel, is associated with the life centers either of a world or of an individual. In the pseudo-Egyptian Tarot the Sphinx is armed with a javelin, and Typhon is being thrown from the wheel. The vertical columns, supporting the wheel and so placed that but one is visible, represent the axis of the world with the inscrutable sphinx upon its northern pole. Sometimes the wheel with its supports is in a boat upon the water. The water is the Ocean of Illusion, which is the sole foundation of the Cycle of Necessity.

The eleventh numbered major trump is called *La Force,* Strength, and portrays a girl wearing a hat in the form of a lemniscate, with her hands upon the mouth of an apparently ferocious lion. Considerable controversy exists as to whether the maid is closing or opening the lion's mouth. Most writers declare her to be closing the jaws of the beast, but a critical inspection conveys the opposite impression. The young woman symbolizes spiritual strength and the lion either the animal world which the girl is mastering or the Secret Wisdom over which she is mistress. The lion also signifies the summer solstice and the girl, Virgo, for when the sun enters this constellation, the Virgin robs the lion of his strength. King Solomon's throne was ornamented with lions and he himself was likened to the king of beasts with the key of wisdom between its teeth. In this sense, the girl may be opening the lion's mouth to find the key contained therein for courage is a prerequisite to the attainment of knowledge. In the pseudo-Egyptian Tarot the symbolism is the same except that the maiden is represented as a priestess wearing an elaborate crown in the form of a bird surmounted by serpents and an ibis.

The twelfth numbered major trump is called *Le Pendu*, the Hanged Man, an portrays a young man hanging by his left leg from a horizontal beam, the latter supported by two tree trunks from each of which six branches have been removed. The right leg of the youth is crossed in back of the left and his arms are folded behind his back in such a way as to form a cross surmounting a downward pointing triangle. The figure thus forms an inverted symbol of sulphur and, according to Levi, signifies the accomplishment of the *magnum opus*. In some decks the figure carries under each arm a money bag from which coins are escaping. Popular tradition associates this card with Judas Iscariot, who is said to have gone forth and hanged himself, the money bags representing the payment he received for his crime.

Levi likens the hanged man to Prometheus, the Eternal Sufferer, further declaring that the upturned feet signify the spiritualization of the lower nature. It is also possible that the inverted figure denotes the loss of the spiritual faculties, for the head is below the level of the body. The stumps of the twelve branches are the signs of the zodiac divided into two groups-- positive and negative. The picture therefore depicts polarity temporarily triumphant over the spiritual principle of equilibrium. To attain the heights of philosophy, therefore, man must reverse (or invert) the order of his life. He then loses his sense of personal possession because he renounces the rule of gold in favor of the golden rule. In the pseudo- Egyptian Tarot the hanged man is suspended between two palm trees and signifies the Sun God who dies perennially for his world.

The thirteenth numbered major trump is called *La Mort*, Death, and portrays a reaping skeleton with a great scythe cutting off the heads, hands, and feet rising out of the earth about it. In the course of its labors the skeleton has apparently cut off one of its own feet. Not all Tarot decks show this peculiarity, but this point well emphasizes the philosophic truth that unbalance and destructiveness are synonymous. The skeleton is the proper emblem of the first and supreme Deity because it is the foundation of the body, as the Absolute is the foundation of creation. The reaping skeleton physically signifies death but philosophically that irresistible impulse in Nature which causes every being to be ultimately absorbed into the divine condition in which it existed before the illusionary universe had been manifested. The blade of the scythe is the moon with its crystallizing power. The field in which death reaps is the universe, and the card discloses that all things growing out of the earth shall be cut down and return to earth again.

Kings, Queens, courtesans, and knaves are alike to death, the master of the visible and apparent parts of all creatures. In some Tarot decks death is symbolized as a figure in armor mounted on a white horse which tramples under foot old and young alike. In the pseudo-Egyptian Tarot a rainbow is seen behind the figure of death, thus signifying that the mortality of the body of itself achieves the immortality of the spirit. Death, though it destroys form, can never destroy life, which continually renews itself. This card is the symbol of the constant renovation of the universe--disintegration that reintegration may follow upon a higher level of expression.

The fourteenth numbered major trump is called *La Temperance,* Temperance, and portrays an angelic figure with the sun upon her forehead. She carries two urns, one empty and the other full, and continually pours the contents of the upper into the lower, In some Tarot decks the flowing water takes the form of the symbol of Aquarius. Not one drop, however, of the living water is lost in this endless transference between the superior vessel and the inferior. When the lower urn is filled the vases are reversed, thus signifying that life pours first from the invisible into the visible, then from the visible back into the invisible. The spirit controlling this flow is an emissary of the great Jehovah, Demiurgus of the world. The sun, or light cluster, upon the woman's forehead controls the flow of water, which, being drawn upward into the air by the solar rays, descends upon the earth as rain, to be drawn up and fall again *ad infinitum*. Herein is also shown the passage of the human life forces back and forth between positive and negative poles of the creative system. In the pseudo-Egyptian Tarot the symbolism is the same, except that the winged figure is male instead of female. It is surrounded by a solar nimbus and pours water from a golden urn into a silver one, typifying the descent of celestial forces into the sublunary spheres.

The fifteenth numbered major trump is called *Le Diable*, the Devil, and portrays a creature resembling Pan with the horns of a ram or deer, the arms and body of a man, and the legs and feet of a goat or dragon. The figure stands upon a cubic stone, to a ring in the front of which are chained two satyrs. For a scepter this so-called demon carries a lighted torch or candle. The entire figure is symbolic of the magic powers of the astral light, or universal mirror, in which the divine forces are reflected in an inverted, or infernal, state. The demon is winged like a bat, showing that it pertains to the nocturnal, or shadow inferior sphere. The animal natures of man, in the form of a male and a female elemental, are chained to its footstool. The torch is the false light which guides unillumined souls to their own undoing. In the pseudo-Egyptian Tarot appears Typhon--a winged creature composed of a hog, a man, a bat, a crocodile, and a hippopotamus--standing in the midst of its own destructiveness and holding aloft the firebrand of the incendiary. Typhon is created by man's own misdeeds, which, turning upon their maker, destroy him.

The sixteenth numbered major trump is called *Le Feu du Ciel,* the Fire of Heaven, and portrays a tower the battlements of which, in the form of a crown, are being destroyed by a bolt of lightning *issuing from the sun.* The crown, being considerably smaller than the tower which it surmounts, possibly indicates that its destruction resulted from its insufficiency. The lighting bolt sometimes takes the form of the zodiacal sign of Scorpio, and the tower may be considered a phallic emblem. Two figures are falling from the tower, one in front and the other behind. This Tarot card is popularly associated with the traditional fall of man. The divine nature of humanity is depicted as a tower. When his crown is destroyed, man falls into the lower world and takes upon himself the illusion of materiality. Here also is a key to the mystery of sex. The tower is supposedly filled with gold coins which, showering out in great numbers from the rent made by the lightning bolt, suggesting potential powers. In the pseudo-Egyptian Tarot the tower is a pyramid, its apex shattered by a lightning bolt. Here is a reference to the missing capstone of the Universal House. In support of Levi's contention that this card is connected with the Hebrew letter *Ayin,* the falling figure in the foreground is similar in general appearance to the sixteenth letter of the Hebrew alphabet.

The seventeenth numbered major trump is called *Les Etoiles,* the Stars, and portrays a young girl kneeling with one foot in water and the other on land, her body somewhat suggesting the swastika. She has two urns, the contents of which she pours upon the land and sea. Above the girl's head are eight stars, one of which is exceptionally large and bright. Count de Gébelin considers the great star to be Sothis or Sirius;

the other seven are the sacred planets of the ancients. He believes the female figure to be Isis in the act of causing the inundations of the Nile which accompanied the rising of the Dog Star. The unclothed figure of Isis may well signify that Nature does not receive her garment of verdure until the rising of the Nile waters releases the germinal life of plants and flowers. The bush and bird (or butterfly) signify the growth and resurrection which accompany the rising of the waters. In the pseudo-Egyptian Tarot the great star contains a diamond composed of a black and white triangle, and the flowering bush is a tall plant with a trifoliate head upon which a butterfly alights. Here Isis is in the form of an upright triangle and the vases have become shallow cups. The elements of water and earth under her feet represent the opposites of Nature sharing impartially in the divine abundance.

The eighteenth numbered major trump is called *La Lune,* the Moon, and portrays Luna rising between two towers--one light and the other dark. A dog and a wolf are baying at the rising moon, and in the foreground is a pool of water from which emerges a crawfish. Between the towers a path winds, vanishing in the extreme background. Court de Gébelin sees in this card another reference to the rising of the Nile and states on the authority of Pausanius that the Egyptians believed the inundations of the Nile to result from the tears of the moon goddess which, falling into the river, swelled its flow. These tears are seen dropping from the lunar face. Court de Gébelin also relates the towers to the Pillars of Hercules, beyond which, according to the Egyptians, the luminaries never passed. He notes also that the Egyptians represented the tropics as dogs who as faithful doorkeepers prevented the sun and moon from penetrating too near the poles. The crab or crawfish signifies the retrograde motion of the moon.

This card also refers to the path of wisdom. Man in his quest of reality emerges from the pool of illusion. After mastering the guardians of the gates of wisdom he passes between the fortresses of science and theology and follows the winding path leading to spiritual liberation. His way is faintly lighted by human reason (the moon), which is but a reflection of divine wisdom. In the pseudo-Egyptian Tarot the towers are pyramids, the dogs are black and white respectively, and the moon is partly obscured by clouds. The entire scene suggests the dreary and desolate place in which the Mystery dramas of the Lesser Rites were enacted.

The nineteenth numbered major trump is called *Le Soleil*, the Sun, and portrays two children--probably Gemini, the Twins--standing together in a garden surrounded by a magic ring of flowers. One of these children should be shown as male and the other female. Behind them is a brick wall apparently enclosing the garden. Above the wall the sun is rising, its rays alternately straight and curved. Thirteen teardrops are falling from the solar face. Levi, seeing in the two children Faith and Reason, which must coexist as long as the temporal universe endures, writes: "Human equilibrium requires two feet, the worlds gravitate by means of two forces, generation needs two sexes. Such is the meaning of the arcanum of Solomon, represented by the two pillars of the temple, Jachin and Boaz." The sun of Truth is shining into the garden of the world over which these two children, as personifications of eternal powers reside. The harmony of the world depends upon the coordination of two qualities symbolized throughout the ages as the mind and the heart. In the pseudo- Egyptian Tarot the children give place to a youth and a maiden. Above them in a solar nimbus is the phallic emblem of generation--a line piercing a circle. Gemini is ruled by Mercury and the two children personify the serpents entwined around the *caduceus*.

The twentieth numbered major trump is called *Le Jugement*, the Judgment, and portrays three figures rising apparently from their tombs, though but one coffin is visible. Above them in a blaze of glory is a winged figure (presumably the Angel Gabriel) blowing a trumpet. This Tarot represents the liberation of man's threefold spiritual nature from the sepulcher of his material constitution. Since but one-third of the spirit actually enters the physical body, the other two-thirds constituting the Hermetic *anthropos* or *overman*, only one of the three figures is actually rising from the tomb. Court de Gébelin believes that the coffin may have been an afterthought of the card makers and that the scene actually represents creation rather than resurrection. In philosophy these two words are practically synonymous. The blast of the trumpet represents the Creative Word, by the intoning of which man is liberated from his terrestrial limitations. In the pseudo-Egyptian Tarot it is evident that the three figures signify the parts of a single being, for three mummies are shown emerging from one mummy case.

The twenty-first numbered major trump is called *Le Monde,* the World, and portrays a female figure draped with a scarf which the wind blows into the form of the Hebrew letter Kaph. Her extended hands-- each of which holds a wand--and her left leg, which crosses behind the right, cause the figure to assume the form of the alchemical symbol of sulphur. The central figure is surrounded by a wreath in the form of a *vesica piscis* which Levi likens to the Qabbalistic crown *Kether.* The Cherubim of Ezekiel's vision occupy the corners of the card. This Tarot is called the Microcosm and the Macrocosm because in it are summed up every agency contributing to the structure of creation. The figure in the form of the emblem of sulphur represents the divine fire and the heart of the Great Mystery. The wreath is Nature, which surrounds the fiery center. The Cherubim represent the elements, worlds, forces, and planes issuing out of the divine fiery center of life. The wreath signifies the crown of the initiate which is given to those who master the four guardians and enter into the presence of unveiled Truth. In the pseudo-Egyptian Tarot the Cherubim surround a wreath composed of twelve trifoliate flowers--the decanates of the zodiac. A human figure kneels below this wreath, playing upon a harp of three strings, for the spirit must create harmony in the triple constitution of its inferior nature before it can gain for itself the solar crown of immortality.

The four suits of the minor trumps are considered as analogous to the four elements, the four corners of creation, and the four worlds of Qabbalism. The key to the lesser Tarots is presumably the *Tetragrammaton,* or the four-letter name of Jehovah, IHVH. The four suits of the minor trumps represent also the major divisions of society: *cups* are the priesthood, *swords* the military, *coins* the tradesmen, and *rods* the farming class. From the standpoint of what Court de Gébelin calls "political geography," *cups* represent the northern countries, *swords* the Orient, *coins* the Occident, and *rods* the southern countries. The ten pip cards of each suit represent the nations composing each of these grand divisions. The *kings* are their governments, the *queens* their religions, the *knights* their histories and national characteristics, and the *pages* their arts and sciences. Elaborate treatises have been written concerning the use of the Tarot cards in divination, but as this practice is contrary to the primary purpose of the Tarot no profit can result from its discussion.

Many interesting examples of early playing cards are found in the museums of Europe, and there are also noteworthy specimens in the cabinets of various private collectors. A few hand-painted decks exist which are extremely artistic. These depict various important personages contemporary with the artists. In some instances, the court cards are portraitures of the reigning monarch and his family. In England engraved cards became popular, and in the British Museum are also to be seen some extremely quaint stenciled cards. Heraldic devices were employed; and Chatto, in his *Origin and History of Playing Cards,* reproduces four heraldic cards in which the arms of Pope Clement IX adorn the king of clubs. There have been philosophical decks with emblems chosen from Greek and Roman mythology, also educational decks ornamented with maps or pictorial representations of famous historic places and incidents. Many rare examples of playing-cards have been found bound into the covers of early books. In Japan there are card games the successful playing of which requires familiarity with nearly all the literary masterpieces of that nation. In India there are circular decks depicting episodes from Oriental myths. There are also cards which in one sense of the word are not cards, for the designs are on wood, ivory, and even metal. There are comic cards caricaturing disliked persons and places, and there are cards commemorating various human achievements. During the American Civil War a patriotic deck was circulated in which stars, eagles, anchors, and American flags were substituted for the suits and the court cards were famous generals.

Modern playing cards are the minor trumps of the Tarot, from each suit of which the *page,* or *valet,* has been eliminated, leaving 13 cards. Even in its abridged form, however, the modern deck is of profound symbolic importance, for its arrangement is apparently in accord with the divisions of the year. The two colors, red and black, represent the two grand divisions of the year--that during which the sun is north of the equator and that during which it is south of the equator. The four suits represent the seasons, the ages of the ancient Greeks, and the *Yugas* of the Hindus. The twelve court cards are the signs of the zodiac arranged in triads of a Father, a Power, and a Mind according to the upper section of the Bembine Table. The ten pip cards of each suit represent the Sephirothic trees existing in each of the four worlds (the suits). The 13 cards of each suit are the 13 lunar months in each year, and the 52 cards of the deck are the 52 weeks in the year. Counting the number of pips and reckoning the jacks, queens, and kings as 11, 12, and 13 respectively, the sum for the 52 cards is 364. If the joker be considered as one point, the result is 365, or the number of days in the year. Milton Pottenger believed that the United States of America was laid out according to the conventional deck of playing cards, and that the government will ultimately consist of 52 States administered by a 53rd undenominated division, the District of Columbia.

The court cards contain a number of important Masonic symbols. Nine are full face and three are profile. Here is the broken "Wheel of the Law," signifying the nine months of the prenatal epoch and the three degrees of spiritual unfoldment necessary to produce the perfect man. The four armed kings are the Egyptian Ammonian Architects who gouged out the universe with knives. They are also the cardinal signs of the zodiac. The four queens, carrying eight-petaled flowers symbolic of the Christ, are the fixed signs of the zodiac. The four jacks, two of whom bear acacia sprigs--the jack of hearts in his hand, the jack of clubs in his hat--are the four common signs of the zodiac. It should be noted also that the court cards of the spade suit will not look upon the pip in the corner of the card but face away from it as though fearing this emblem of death. The Grand Master of the Order of the Cards is the king of clubs, who carries the orb as emblematic of his dignity.

www.ingramcontent.com/pod-product-compliance
Lightning Source LLC
LaVergne TN
LVHW041459070426
835507LV00009B/695